Personality Patterns

Quiz Book

by Alice Oglethorpe
illustrations by Shannon Laskey

★ American Girl®

Questions or comments? Call 1-800-845-0005,
visit **americangirl.com**, or write to Customer Service,
American Girl, 8400 Fairway Place, Middleton, WI 53562-0497.

Printed in China
13 14 15 16 17 18 19 20 LEO 10 9 8 7 6 5 4 3 2 1

Editorial Development: Carrie Anton
Art Direction & Design: Lisa Wilber
Production: Tami Kepler, Janell Wisecup, Paula Moon, Judith Lary
Illustrations: Shannon Laskey

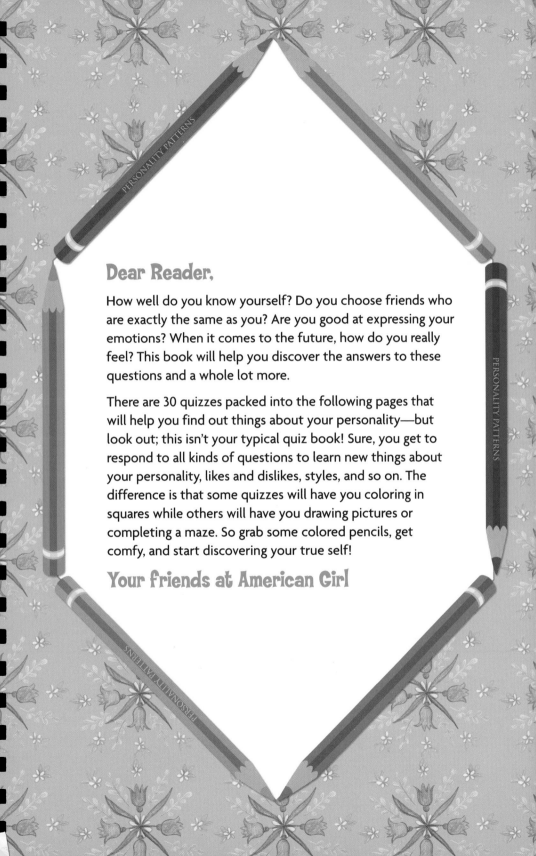

Dear Reader,

How well do you know yourself? Do you choose friends who are exactly the same as you? Are you good at expressing your emotions? When it comes to the future, how do you really feel? This book will help you discover the answers to these questions and a whole lot more.

There are 30 quizzes packed into the following pages that will help you find out things about your personality—but look out; this isn't your typical quiz book! Sure, you get to respond to all kinds of questions to learn new things about your personality, likes and dislikes, styles, and so on. The difference is that some quizzes will have you coloring in squares while others will have you drawing pictures or completing a maze. So grab some colored pencils, get comfy, and start discovering your true self!

Your friends at American Girl

Table of Contents

Social or Solo?

Discover whether you're happiest surrounded by others or prefer doing your own thing. For each question, color in one square with the specified color—the key at the end will hold the answer!

You wake up in the morning to hear that it's a snow day.
No school! After celebrating, which do you do?

Color one square **pink**
if you send a text to all of
your friends to schedule
a huge snowball fight.

Color one square **blue**
if you ask your sister
or next-door neighbor to
build a snowman together.

Color one square **yellow**
if you make a mug of hot
cocoa and curl up
with a book and a blanket.

It's a gorgeous Saturday and you want to do something outside.
Which of the following do you decide to do?

Color one square **pink**
if you go to the park to
see if anyone is playing
kickball or basketball.

Color one square **blue**
if you find a friend to
pair up with for a game of
tennis or to play catch.

Color one square **yellow**
if you play fetch with your
dog in the backyard.

You received a bad grade on your math test, and later the teacher
told you to quiet down. To vent, what do you do?

Color one square **pink**
if you tell as many of
your friends as possible
what happened.

Color one square **blue**
if you call your BFF after
school, hoping she'll
boost your mood.

Color one square **yellow**
if you whip out your
journal and start
writing away.

In the yearbook, where is someone most likely to find pictures of you?

Color one square **pink**
if there are photos of
you on almost every page
thanks to all the clubs and
teams you joined.

Color one square **blue**
if there are photos of you
sprinkled here and
there a few times.

Color one square **yellow**
if you make your only
appearance in the
class headshot.

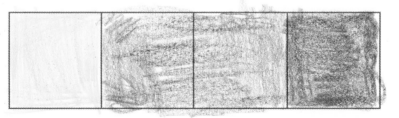

Your mom takes away your phone privileges as a punishment. How do you feel?

Color one square **pink** if you are devastated. After all, how are you going to find out what all your friends did after school?

Color one square **blue** if you are frustrated. It's hard to make plans without a phone!

Color one square **yellow** if you're only slightly bummed. You don't use the phone all that much anyway.

Over summer vacation, you go with your parents to visit your grandparents for a week. What do you do while you're there?

Color one square **pink** if you walk up and introduce yourself to the kids you see playing outside near your grandparents' house.

Color one square **blue** if you have a blast with your cousins or siblings.

Color one square **yellow** if you read books, go on walks, and generally stick to yourself.

What are you most likely to do after swim practice?

Color one square **pink** if you beg to hang out with the team longer —everyone is going to be playing at the pool for an hour.

Color one square **blue** if you ask your mom if you can go hang out at a friend's house until dinner.

Color one square **yellow** if you head home to put the finishing touches on the craft you've been making.

Which of the following best describes what you do when your science teacher assigns a group project?

Color one square **pink** if you think about how fun it's going to be to use homework as a reason to hang out with your friends.

Color one square **blue** if you hope you aren't stuck with people you don't know very well.

Color one square **yellow** if you suggest that the group divvy up the tasks and work separately on the different pieces.

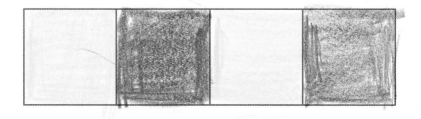

Answers

Think Pink: If you colored in more pink squares, you're a social butterfly! Whenever you get the chance, you'd rather be surrounded by lots of people. You feel comfortable talking to anyone and have loads of friends. Always having someone around is a great support system, but don't forget that some downtime alone can be good when you need a break.

Blue Is for You: If you colored in more blue squares, then you like hanging out with your close group of friends. You have a lot of fun being social, but you can be a little quiet at times. That's why you feel more comfortable when your group is on the smaller side.

Yay for Yellow: If you colored in more yellow squares, you enjoy doing things on your own a lot of the time. You don't hate being social, but you also don't feel a need to fill every spare moment with activities involving other people. If you're ever starting to feel a little lonely, reach out to a friend to see if she wants to do something you usually enjoying doing alone, such as drawing, jumping rope, or solving a jigsaw puzzle.

Room for You

Your room is where you sleep, study, and sometimes socialize, and it can reveal a lot about your personality. Set a timer for one minute, look around your room, and put an X over things you see on the board below. You'll never look at your bedroom the same way again!

F	U	N
framed artwork ✓	pile of messy clothes ✓	something with your name on it ✓
decorative pillows ✓	unmade bed	photos of you and your friends ✓
candles ✓	books out of place ✓	a piece of your own artwork ✓
vases	random pieces of paper ✓	a DIY project you made ✓
pretty curtains	an old drinking glass	something from a thrift store ✓

Answers

If you filled up more of the **F** column, then you're really into **interior design.** You have an eye for style and like playing around with different looks in your room. Ask your mom or dad to get you some decorating magazines (or check out your local library's selection)—you'll feel inspired to try something new!

If you filled up more of the **U** column, you **don't really care about how your room looks.** You don't spend much time picking things up or putting them away. As an experiment, try a five-minute cleanup challenge every night. You'll be surprised at the difference a little time spent cleaning can make.

If you filled up more of the **N** column, you love **making things your own.** Whether you put pictures of your friends everywhere, make your own cool décor, or search for that one perfect piece, you can rest assured that nobody else's room looks like yours.

Clean Machine

In the game of life, there are Neat Nancys and Cluttered Clares. To find out which one you are, fill in four squares wherever you want on the grid below. The pattern will clue you in to how much order is in your life.

Answers

If you put the squares all in one line or evenly spaced out, you like things nice and neat. You probably don't have any trouble keeping your room clean, and you put clothes away as soon as they're out of the dryer.

If your squares are clustered together, you tend to be a piler. Random messy piles could mean you need a little more order in your life. Piles of similar items mean you like to know where everything is—but that doesn't necessarily mean your belongings always make it to their rightful places.

If your squares are scattered all around the grid, staying super tidy is not a priority for you. It's fine if you tend to be a little messy, but try to at least keep important things such as your schoolwork and supplies neat—knowing where your science notes are will save you time and help you score an A on the next test!

'Tis the Season

Some people live for sunny summer days, while others can't wait for winter wonderlands. Learn if you're happiest in hot or cold weather by filling in the thermometer for each question.

Which sport do you like better?
If ice-skating, fill it in a little.
If swimming, fill it in a lot.

What do you like wearing more?
If sweaters, fill it in a little.
If shorts, fill it in a lot.

What do you like to have on your feet?
If boots, fill it in a little.
If flip-flops, fill it in a lot.

  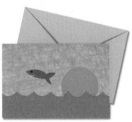

Where would you rather visit?
If the mountains, fill it in a little.
If the beach, fill it in a lot.

Which activity do you like better?
If sledding, fill it in a little.
If tubing down a waterslide, fill it in a lot.

Which drink is your favorite?
If hot cocoa, fill it in a little.
If lemonade, fill it in a lot.

For dessert, which would you pick?
If freshly baked cookies, fill it in a little.
If ice cream, fill it in a lot.

Which would you rather build?
If a snowman, fill it in a little.
If a sand castle, fill it in a lot.

What are your favorite colors?
If blues, greens, and purples, fill it in a little.
If reds, oranges, and yellows, fill it in a lot.

Answers

If most of the thermometers read low, you're a fall and winter person! You like the smell of crisp air, the crunch of leaves under your feet, and bundling up to play in the snow.

If the mercury in your thermometers is on the rise, you're a spring and summer person! You love to see the flowers and you love summer vacation, when you can spend all day at the pool.

If the temperature differences are too close to call, you're a four-season girl. Why pick a favorite when each one has something spectacular to offer?

Stargazing

If you could have anything in the world, what would it be? Find out what your deepest desire is by looking at this picture of a starry sky and deciding what the first shape you see is.

Answers

If you saw a heart first, you wish deep down to be always surrounded by your closest friends. Consider your wish granted! While you may meet other girls, if you work hard at staying in touch with your current BFFs, you'll always stay close.

If you saw a book first, your deepest wish is to become a successful career woman. Keep studying in school, and you're sure to be a star at whatever job you choose.

If you saw a tennis racket first, you really want to become a world-class athlete. Practice as much as you can and ask your coaches for pointers—there's no reason why it can't happen!

If you saw an airplane first, you long to be a world traveler. Start by exploring your own town and state with your family. By the time you're older, you'll be a pro at packing and will feel comfortable in new places.

If you saw a horse first, your wish is to have lots of animals in your life. Even if you don't want to live on a farm, you can still have a career that works with animals, such as becoming a veterinarian. Just make sure to pay attention in science class!

If you saw a flag on a pole first, you deep down want to become President of the United States. Study, volunteer a lot, and run for your class government. Shoot for the stars!

If you saw a smile first, your wish is to help those less fortunate than you are. Start small by collecting canned food for your local food pantry or used towels for an animal shelter. Or find out what needs your community is facing and help there. One little action can make a huge difference!

PLAY Away

You can fit a lot of fun into a year, and how you choose to spend your time can say a lot about your personality. Set a timer for one minute and put an X over every activity that you've done in the past year to find out what your hobbies say about you.

P	L	A	Y
tubing on a river	crocheting	kickball	painting
horse-back riding	making jewelry	soccer	pottery
skate-boarding	origami	basketball	photo-graphy
skiing/snow-boarding	making collages	swimming	drawing
hiking	sewing	softball	playing an instrument

Mostly Ps: You are up for adventures and like to push yourself to try new things. You love feeling a rush of adrenaline and knowing that you conquered a new activity. Make sure to always be careful, though. Ask your parent for permission, and always wear protective gear, such as a helmet.

Mostly Ls: You like staying inside and finding new crafts to do at home. You're often found at a table, hard at work with your supplies all around you. If you want to try something new, take a stroll through a craft store or look in the hobby section at the library. There will be books with step-by-step instructions for all sorts of creative projects.

Mostly As: If there's an organized sport out there, you've probably played it. You love being active and are willing to give any type of sport a try. If there's a specific one you like the most, see if there's a summer camp that specializes in it. You'll get to learn a lot of new skills and meet other girls who share your passion.

Mostly Ys: You're artistic and like to do things that push your creativity. You love to doodle, sketch, paint, and draw. Check the library for books about famous art styles. You'll learn about what inspired them.

Inner Color

The colors you're drawn to can say a lot about your energy. See for yourself by coloring in the boxes using any colors you want.

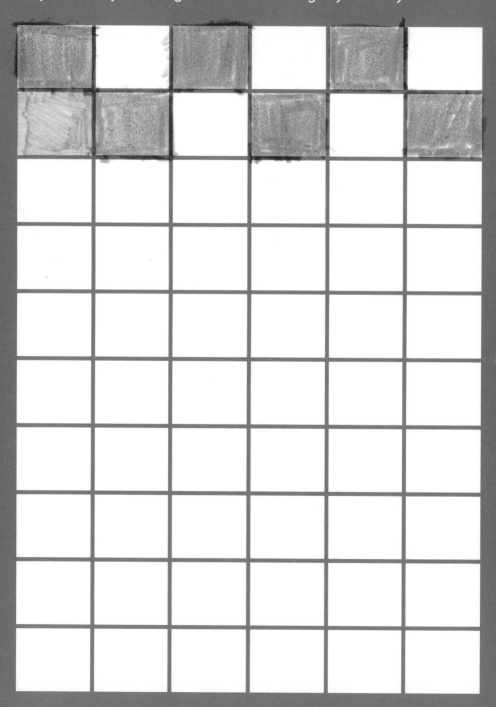

Answers

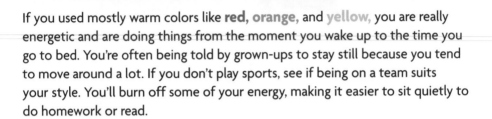

If you used mostly warm colors like **red, orange,** and yellow, you are really
energetic and are doing things from the moment you wake up to the time you
go to bed. You're often being told by grown-ups to stay still because you tend
to move around a lot. If you don't play sports, see if being on a team suits
your style. You'll burn off some of your energy, making it easier to sit quietly to
do homework or read.

If you used mostly cool colors like **blue, green,** and **purple,** you are pretty mellow
and don't get super worked up about things. You can sit quietly by yourself reading or doing schoolwork, and on weekends you sometimes need to be forced to
play out of the house. The good thing about your personality is that you stay calm
when others may get upset about something. That cool head will help you
a lot in life.

If you used a **rainbow** of colors, you alternate between having tons of energy and
being more low-key. Some days you can go, go, go without resting; others you want
to spend on the sofa chilling out with a movie. Split your day into chunks so that
half the day is spent being active and half is spent at home catching up on schoolwork and reading. It's the best of both worlds!

Creature Characteristics

Sure, you're human, but everybody has a little bit of an animal inside. Using the letters in the word **elephant,** come up with a three-letter animal. Then find out what that word says about you!

Answers

If your first word was **EEL**, it means you are good at figuring out unique solutions to tough problems. You know that even though a situation seems difficult, there's always an answer!

If your first word was **ANT**, it means you're a hard worker who knows the joy of putting in lots of time and effort on something and having it turn out really well.

If your first word was **APE**, it means you love being a leader. While this is a great trait, don't forget to let others call the shots sometimes. Being able to work in a group is an important skill, too!

If your first word was **HEN**, it means you are very nurturing and like to fuss over others to make sure they're happy. Don't stretch yourself too thin. Your own happiness is just as important, if not more so!

23

Wow the World

Do you have what it takes to become a five-star chef? A lead singer in a rock-and-roll band? A Nobel Prize winner? Discover more about your talents by coloring in a flower in the vase on the foldout page as instructed in each question.

1. What do you like best to do on weekend mornings?
Color a flower **red** if you like to eat a yummy breakfast.
Color a flower **yellow** if you listen to music in your room.
Color a flower **purple** if you catch up on updating your diary.

2. Which of the following is your favorite subject in school?
Color a flower **red** for home economics.
Color a flower **yellow** for music.
Color a flower **purple** for English.

3. If you are in charge of the remote, what do you flip to first on TV?
Color a flower **red** for cooking contests.
Color a flower **yellow** for singing contests.
Color a flower **purple** for comedies.

4. Which of the following guessing games sounds like the most fun to play?
Color a flower **red** to guess what ingredients are in a dish.
Color a flower **yellow** to guess what instruments are being played in a song.
Color a flower **purple** to guess what unfamiliar words mean.

5. What are your favorite new things to explore?
   Color a flower **red** for restaurants and recipes.
   Color a flower **yellow** for types of music
   and bands.
   Color a flower **purple** for books and authors.

6. Your older cousin is getting married and you're
   invited. What are you most excited about?
   Color a flower **red** if you can't wait to see and
   taste the wedding cake.
   Color a flower **yellow** if you can't wait
   to dance all night long.
   Color a flower **purple** if you can't wait to
   hear the vows the bride and groom have
   written for each other.

7. What fills the pages of your scrapbook?
   Color a flower **red** if it's packed with recipes you'd
   like to try.
   Color a flower **yellow** if it has pages of concert
   ticket stubs.
   Color a flower **purple** if you stuck in notes you
   and your friends have written to each other.

8. What is your favorite part of doing an experiment
   in science class?
   Color a flower **red** if it's mixing the chemicals.
   Color a flower **yellow** if it's following the
   instructions.
   Color a flower **purple** if you like writing down
   the results.

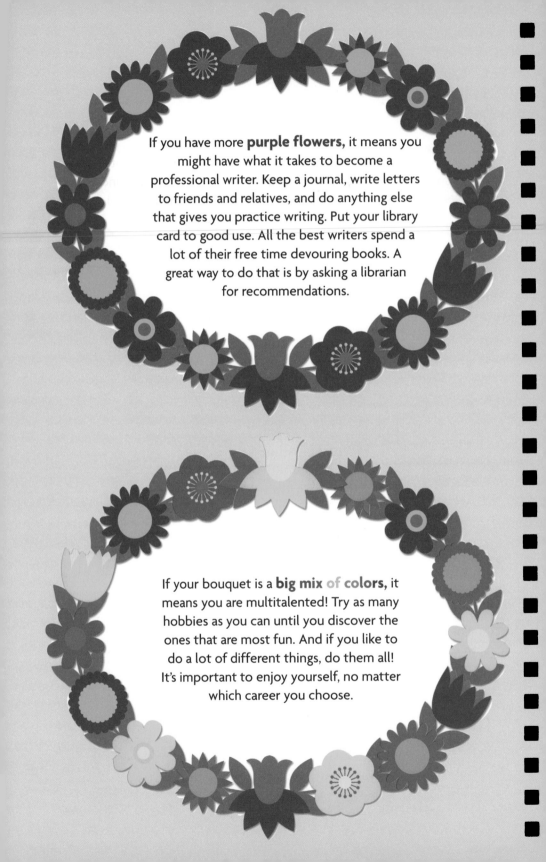

If you have more **purple flowers,** it means you might have what it takes to become a professional writer. Keep a journal, write letters to friends and relatives, and do anything else that gives you practice writing. Put your library card to good use. All the best writers spend a lot of their free time devouring books. A great way to do that is by asking a librarian for recommendations.

If your bouquet is a **big mix of colors,** it means you are multitalented! Try as many hobbies as you can until you discover the ones that are most fun. And if you like to do a lot of different things, do them all! It's important to enjoy yourself, no matter which career you choose.

Answers

If you have more **red flowers,** it means you might make a great chef. Ask your parents if you can start helping out with dinner and experimenting with different flavor combinations. When you get to high school, think about getting a job at a local restaurant. You'll see what really goes into making a restaurant run and find out if you have what it takes to go pro.

If you have more yellow flowers, it means you should try playing an instrument. It can be something classic, such as a clarinet, or something a little more edgy, such as the drums. If your school doesn't have a band you can join, ask your parents if you can take lessons. Try listening to as many different styles of music as you can. There's a lot more out there than pop!

Style Scheme

Would other people label your look as more bohemian, modern, or preppy? Pick one answer for each question and see how your tastes come together.

1. What color shirt do you wear most often?

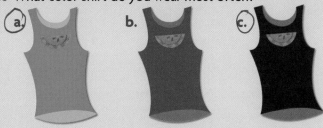

a.   b.   c.

2. What pattern wallpaper would you want in your room?

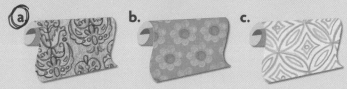

a.   b.   c.

3. Which shape pendant would you buy to wear on a necklace?

a.   b.   c.

4. In what color paper do you like to wrap gifts?

a.   b.   c.

5. Pick your favorite dress pattern.

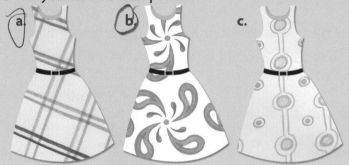

6. With what color pen do you most like to write?

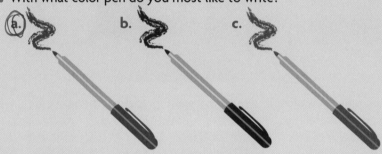

7. What pattern do you doodle most often?

8. Which shape purse is your favorite?

Answers

Preppy Pride

If you chose more **a's**, you like to wear pastels and love cute animal prints. For a fun look, mix your polo shirts and pink clothing with something a little edgy, such as cool print sneakers.

Bohemian Best

If you chose more **b's**, you're a hippie at heart and love all things retro. Thrift and vintage stores are great places to find one-of-a-kind pieces!

Mad for Modern

If you chose more **c's**, you're cutting-edge in your style and are always wearing the latest trends. Don't be afraid to make the look your own—you want to stay true to who you are!

Weekend Fun Forecast

Find a parent or grandparent for this quiz. Write your name above the top circle and the other person's name below the bottom circle. Using the list of hobbies given, write the ones only you like to do in your section, the ones only the other person likes to do in his or her section, and the ones you both enjoy in the middle section. If there is something on the list that neither of you likes, skip it and move on to the next. Once you're done, pick a weekend to do some of the activities in the middle together! And check out the answer key to learn what your finished diagram says about you.

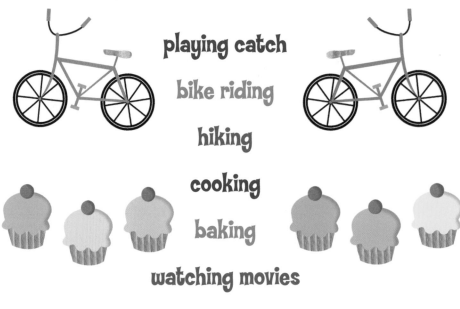

playing catch

bike riding

hiking

cooking

baking

watching movies

taking pictures

drawing

painting

gardening

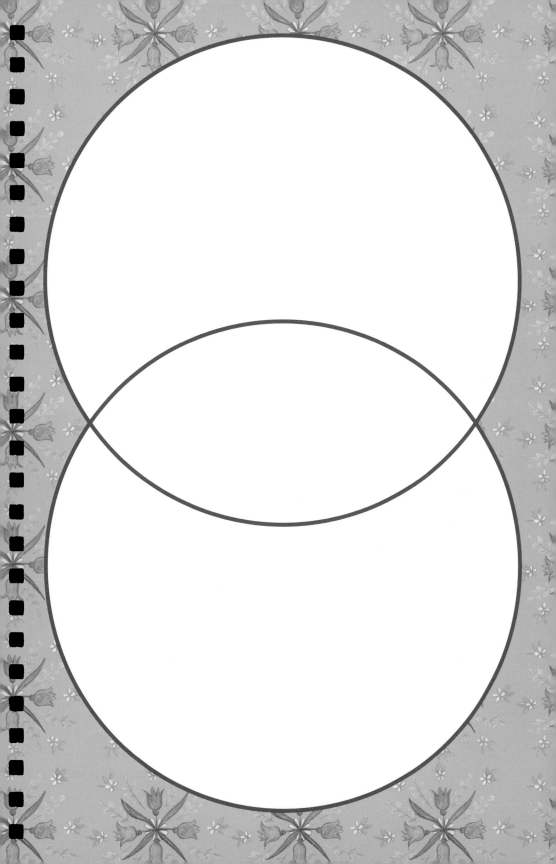

Answers

If the words in the middle are mostly **active things,** it means you both like to get up and go on the weekends! Make sure you eat a healthful snack first, such as a banana and peanut butter sandwich. You'll have lots of energy to stay on the move all day long.

If the words in the middle are mostly **things done in the home,** it means you two tend to stay inside to have fun. For a fun Sunday dinner, pick a theme—such as Italian or barbecue—and plan an entire meal around it.

If the words in the middle are mostly **artsy things,** it means you two are clever and creative. Get your hands messy together while trying something you've never done before—even if it's something silly like finger painting!

If the words in the middle are **a mix of all kinds of activities,** you two are up for anything! Don't be overwhelmed by all the possibilities—just pick the activity that sounds the most fun and do it this weekend. Then sprinkle the other activities throughout the coming months. You two will have a blast!

Hide-and-Secrets

You may say you feel fine when a parent asks you about school, your friends, and the future. But do you really? Find three words hidden in the following puzzle and jot them down in the order you found them. They will unveil what secret emotions you really have. (Note: Words can be found in any direction.)

```
M  V  T  A  Y  H  T  C  R  R
F  C  E  D  Q  E  E  A  X  C
W  Q  D  H  Q  K  S  L  T  E
G  I  G  O  O  D  P  M  V  S
G  L  I  X  I  K  U  B  R  L
A  L  A  Z  L  L  G  P  Z  F
D  K  X  D  G  R  C  J  W  H
I  W  X  S  W  B  E  S  O  E
H  W  Q  L  N  V  H  X  W  Q
D  P  I  B  V  Y  P  P  A  H
G  E  L  L  T  Y  H  S  V  S
A  A  R  O  H  A  F  S  U  S
H  Q  I  O  Q  J  N  L  I  O
E  W  U  A  B  O  T  J  Z  A
```

Answers

The **first word** you found shows how you feel about your friends. Ideally it was a positive word, but if not, maybe there is something a little off. Try figuring out what it is and talking to your friends about it. If they care about you, they will work on fixing the problem.

The **second word** you found shows how you feel about school. If things are going well, stay the course. If you aren't that happy, talk to a favorite teacher or your parents. They might have some ideas to make it a better place for you!

The **third word** you found shows how you feel about your future. Is it exciting and great or a little scary? You have your whole life in front of you, and such wonderful things are going to happen. Focus on all the good things coming up for you, and you'll instantly feel more excited.

Goofy Girl

Some people are silly all the time, while others tend to be more serious. To find out how goofy you are, use the space below to draw a dog in any type of pose you choose.

Answers

If the dog is standing or running, it means you have a serious silly side. You have a great sense of humor and get a kick out of playing lighthearted practical jokes. Some people consider you the class clown. It's fun to make people laugh, but comedy is all about timing. Maybe wait until after class to tell your joke.

If the dog is sitting, it means you can be goofy from time to time. You know when to crack a joke and when to be a bit more serious. This is a great trait because you rarely get into trouble for acting up when you shouldn't. If you're ever in doubt about how you should behave, ask one of your parents. They're more mature and have a better idea about how to act.

If the dog is lying down, it means you tend to be on the serious side. Don't be afraid to do silly things every now and then—laughing is one of the best things you can do! And don't worry: You don't have to be the one making the jokes. Instead, watch cartoons and read silly books. They'll always put you in a good mood.

Future Picasso

Some people are super creative, while others tend to be more on the logical side. Follow the instructions given in each set of questions and answers. At the end, you'll discover how artistic you are.

1. Which is your favorite activity in art class?

Draw a **circle** around the question number if you like getting your hands messy with paint and sticky supplies.

Draw a **star** around the question number if you enjoy cutting out collage pictures from magazines.

Draw a **triangle** around the question number if you prefer to organize by color the pencils and markers in your art case.

2. When it's your mom's birthday, which one are you most likely to do?

Draw a **circle** around the question number if you make her a card from scratch.

Draw a **star** around the question number if you write a poem for her in a store-bought card.

Draw a **triangle** around the question number if you write "I love you!" in a store-bought card.

3. It's time for a dad-and-daughter meal. How do you help him out?

Draw a **circle** around the question number if you start measuring and mixing without even reading the recipe.

Draw a **star** around the question number if you read over the recipe but add a dash of a favorite spice not called for in the recipe.

Draw a **triangle** around the question number if you follow the recipe exactly.

4. Which of the following best describes how you get dressed in the morning?

Draw a **circle** around the question number if you mix and match as many colors and patterns as you can.

Draw a **star** around the question number if you think about how different clothes go together before putting together your outfit.

Draw a **triangle** around the question number if you dress in a specific color according to what day it is.

5. Your English teacher asks you to write an essay about your dream career. Which one do you pick?

Draw a **circle** around the question number if you opt to be an interior designer.

Draw a **star** around the question number if you choose to be a journalist.

Draw a **triangle** around the question number if you want to be a doctor.

6. Which of the following are your favorite things to read?

Draw a **circle** around the question number if you like to read graphic novels or comic books.

Draw a **star** around the question number if you go for imaginative stories about made-up worlds.

Draw a **triangle** around the question number if you choose stories about girls who remind you of yourself.

7. You are helping a younger sister or cousin work on a coloring book. Which one best describes your approach?

Draw a **circle** around the question number if you add all kinds of extra detail to the page illustration.

Draw a **star** around the question number if you make up a story about the picture you're coloring.

Draw a **triangle** around the question number if you focus your attention on staying perfectly within the lines.

8. Which prize would you most like to win?

Draw a **circle** around the question number if you would love to take home an Oscar for best art direction in a movie.

Draw a **star** around the question number if you would be honored to receive a Pulitzer Prize for best novel.

Draw a **triangle** around the question number if you dream of a Nobel Prize for your work in finding a cure for a disease.

Answers

More circles?
You're super creative!
You're a budding painter or illustrator, and you might have a future in the arts. Try taking extra classes after school or during the summer to improve your skills. And don't forget to always keep a sketch pad nearby.

More stars?
You are creative and prefer to express yourself through writing. The best way to become a better writer is to read a lot, so keep using your library card!

More triangles?
You tend to be more logical in your thinking and like having a set of instructions to follow. Think about signing up for the science club or math team to meet others who have similar interests. Get out with Mom or Dad on exploration hikes where you can learn more about the intricate world around you.

Sports Star

Just because you aren't the captain of your soccer team doesn't mean you don't have an inner athlete waiting to come out. For each question, shade in the water bottle from 0 to 5. Leave the bottle empty if you disagree completely with the statement, fill it to 5 if you completely agree, or go in between. ← 5

← 0

You play on a sports team.

You have a favorite female athlete.

You like to watch sports on TV.

You love gym class.

You own a T-shirt with a team name on it.

You usually get picked first for teams.

You often join in neighborhood games of kickball or tag.

You're usually wearing sneakers.

When you're stressed, you do something physical to feel better.

You don't mind getting sweaty.

You're rarely sitting down.

You have more sneakers than any other kind of shoes.

Your favorite thing to do at recess is shoot hoops or jump rope.

You can do a cartwheel.

Your hair is often kept out of your face in a ponytail or braids or with an elastic headband.

Answers

If most of the **water bottles are full,** you're ready to play in the game. You're a natural athlete and shouldn't be afraid to try out for a team with the other girls.

If most of the **water bottles are in the middle,** you like some sports but not all of them. It's good to be active, so try out a few different sports or games to get you moving until you find one or two you like the most.

If most of the **water bottles are low or empty,** maybe sports aren't your thing. But don't skip out on being active. Go for walks with your parents, play hopscotch in the driveway, and give your little brother piggyback rides around the backyard.

Scaredy Cat

Ghosts, bumps in the night, and pop quizzes aren't the only things that can be frightening! Find out your own fears by deciding what kind of animal you see in the paint blot below.

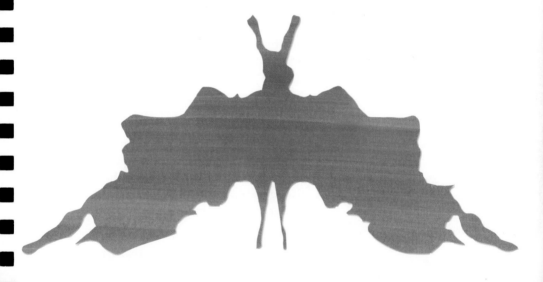

Answers

If you saw a **bird,** it means you're afraid of leaving home. While it can be scary to think that one day you're going to be old enough to go off on your own, by the time that point in your life comes around, you're going to be ready! And remember: You only have to go as far away as you feel comfortable going.

If you saw a **bat,** it means you're afraid of what you can't see. When it's dark outside and you can't tell where certain noises are coming from, it's natural to feel scared! Just remind yourself what the world looks like with the sun shining and that it's the same place, just with a little less light.

If you saw a **butterfly,** it means you're afraid of change. Most people are scared when things in their lives start changing, but it's impossible for everything to stay the same forever. Try to relax and go with the flow—soon the new things will feel as if they've always been that way.

Stumped and **can't see anything?** You aren't afraid of much at all! You have a brave attitude and feel excited when you're facing the unknown. You deserve a round of applause for your adventurous spirit, but make sure to be a little cautious when it's called for. And know that it's OK if you ever do feel frightened about the future or change—it's a completely natural feeling and will go away in time.

Say Cheese!

What are some of the things that really lift your spirits? Pick out three of your favorite photographs that you've taken over the past year. Got them? Now look at them and discover what those images say about you.

Answers

If the photos show your **friends,** you love being with your BFFs as much as you can. Whether it's hanging out in someone's bedroom, eating lunch together at school, or exploring the mall on the weekends, your friends know you the best, and you know you can be yourself around them.

If the photos show **vacations,** being on adventures makes you happy. It could be exploring a new part of your hometown or going to an exciting new destination with your family over the summer, but as long as you're seeing new places, you're smiling.

If the photos show **animals and landscapes,** being one with nature makes you happy. You love being surrounded by trees, smelling fresh air, and feeling the grass or sand between your toes.

Scoops of Emotion

Are you super sappy, or do you tend to keep your emotions tucked away inside? Find out by coloring in a scoop of ice cream on the cone for each question.

1. When you write notes to your friends, how do you end them?

Color a **chocolate scoop** if you simply sign your name.

Color a **strawberry scoop** if you end with "XOXO."

Color an **orange sherbet scoop** if you use "BFFs forever."

2. What do you do to help cheer up your sister after she's had a really bad day?

Color a **chocolate scoop** if you let her pick what TV show to watch—even if it's your turn to choose.

Color a **strawberry scoop** if you make her laugh by telling her a funny story.

Color an **orange sherbet scoop** if you tell her everything that you think is great about her.

3. After two weeks away at summer camp, you see your parents for the first time. What do you do?

Color a **chocolate scoop** if you show them the cool arts-and-crafts projects you did.

Color a **strawberry scoop** if you give them a hug and then take them on a tour of your cabin.

Color an **orange sherbet scoop** if you run to them and tell them how much you missed them.

4. A good friend's grandmother passed away. What do you do?

Color a **chocolate scoop** if you give her some quiet time and don't really say much about it.

Color a **strawberry scoop** if you tell her that you're there for her if she needs anything at all.

Color an **orange sherbet scoop** if you write her a special note telling her how sorry you are for her.

5. On the last day of school, what do you give your favorite teacher?

Color a **chocolate scoop** if you give her a high five.

Color a **strawberry scoop** if you give her some nice-smelling hand lotion.

Color an **orange sherbet scoop** if you give her a thank-you note for everything she did for you during the year.

6. How often do you tell your parents that you love them?

Color a **chocolate scoop** if it's about once or twice a month.

Color a **strawberry scoop** if it's about once or twice a week.

Color an **orange sherbet scoop** if it's about once or twice a day.

7. After the holidays, how do you respond when your mom tells you to write thank-you notes to your relatives?

Color a **chocolate scoop** if you change the subject.

Color a **strawberry scoop** if you get right to it.

Color an **orange sherbet scoop** if you tell her you're already done.

Chocolate Sensation

You tend to keep a lot of your emotions inside. Think about why you don't express them that often. Are you afraid of being made fun of? Remind yourself that people love to hear your sweet thoughts and that it will only make your relationships stronger. Start off by writing down in a letter how you feel—it's easier than saying something face-to-face.

Super Strawberry

You often show that you're happy to see someone or how much you care, but you have a harder time saying the words. That's totally normal. If you have something nice you want to say to someone, just blurt it out without thinking too much about it. You'll see that the person will appreciate what you said, and you'll get more comfortable doing it.

Oodles of Orange

You're great at expressing your emotions! When you feel love or pride about someone close to you, you make sure to let them know! As a result, your friends and family will know how much they mean to you and will tell you how important you are to them, too. It's a wonderful cycle.

Chill Out

Everybody needs to have ways to wind down. Pick your three favorite images and then turn the page to discover what you can do to feel less stressed or anxious!

If you picked the **book,** grab a fun novel or magazine and lose yourself in its pages.

If you picked the **bar of soap,** take a soak in a bath full of bubbles.

If you picked the **musical notes,** hit the "play" button on some dance songs and get moving around your room.

If you picked the **sneakers,** get sweaty! Grab a hula hoop, soccer ball, or flying disc and get a parent or sibling or friend to play with you.

If you picked the **laughing mouth,** find something to make you giggle. Read a joke book or watch a funny show on TV.

HA-HA-HA!

ha-ha-ha!

If you picked the **pen and piece of paper,** write down five things that made you happy today. You'll instantly be smiling.

If you picked the **board game,** play a game with your family after dinner. You'll lose yourself in the friendly competition.

If you picked the **box of crayons,** do something artistic, such as coloring in a book or drawing something you're thinking about.

If you picked the **phone,** talk to someone about your feelings: It can be your best friend, sister, mom, or dad or anyone with whom you're close.

Super Powered

You may not be able to fly or become invisible, but everyone has special talents. Do you know what yours are? In the grid below, fill in as many of the circles as you'd like in order to create a picture of something. The key at the end will shine a light on one of your strongest skills!

Answers

If you drew a flower, tree, or other nature-inspired image, you are sweet and will bend over backward to help those you care about. With a personality like that, you'll always have lots of friends throughout your life. And don't be afraid to ask favors of other people sometimes when you really need them—life is all about giving and receiving.

If you drew something that's more abstract or geometric, like a building, you're a hard worker who can accomplish anything you set your mind to. Use that strength to come up with some pretty wild goals: joining a rock band, becoming an astronaut, discovering a cure for cancer. You have no idea what you can accomplish unless you try!

If you drew a person or animal, you are a kind girl who is really good at listening to others and helping them see a solution to their problems. With those strengths, you could become a counselor or teacher when you're older. In the meantime, remember that when a friend complains to you about a tough situation, don't put pressure on yourself to fix it. Every now and then, people just like to vent.

Boredom Buster

Try this activity the next time you find yourself at home on a nice day with nothing to do. Instead of moping around or watching TV all day, try something fun. But what? Using the letters in the word **house**, come up with a new four-letter word. Then use that word to see how you should fill your day.

Sunny Side Up or Down

For every situation, you can choose to focus on the positive or the negative. To see how sunny your disposition is, answer each question and draw the appropriate number of clouds in the sky on the next page.

1. What do you usually think after taking a test?

Don't draw any clouds if you think, "I nailed it!"

Draw one cloud if you think, "That was tough, but I think I did OK."

Draw two clouds if you think, "Oh man, I did horrible."

2. Which do you assume before dress shopping?

Don't draw any clouds if you think that you're going to find the perfect dress.

Draw one cloud if you think you're going to have to try on a lot of dresses before finding one you might like.

Draw two clouds if you think it's going to be impossible to find a dress you like that's within your budget.

3. Your class is holding elections for school government. Which of the following do you do?

Don't draw any clouds if you run for president—you're sure you could win!

Draw one cloud if you get talked into running for vice president.

Draw two clouds if you couldn't imagine ever running for a position.

4. How do you feel the night before the first day of school?

Don't draw any clouds if you're excited about all the possibilities.

Draw one cloud if you're a little nervous about starting a new grade.

Draw two clouds if you're worried about how hard the work is going to be.

5. After drawing a picture, to whom do you decide to show it?

Don't draw any clouds if you show it off to your parents and ask them to put it up on the refrigerator.

Draw one cloud if you decide to show a close friend and hang it up in your room.

Draw two clouds if you keep it tucked away.

6. You find out that your best friend is moving far away. What now?

Don't draw any clouds if you know that you'll keep in touch and stay close despite the distance.

Draw one cloud if you worry the two of you may drift apart, but intend to try your hardest to not let that happen.

Draw two clouds if you decide you need a new best friend since it's too hard to keep in touch miles apart.

7. Your mom asks if you want to start a little garden in your backyard. How do you respond?

Don't draw any clouds if you say, "Of course!" Who knows—you just might discover your green thumb.

Draw one cloud if you tell her you will as long as she helps you. Left on your own, you may not be able to get anything to grow.

Draw two clouds if you decide to pass. You've never gardened before—chances are you won't be able to grow more than weeds.

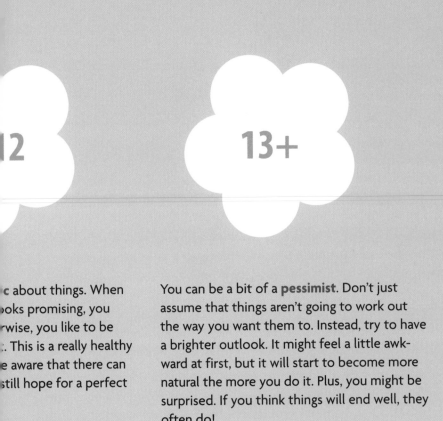

12

13+

c about things. When
oks promising, you
rwise, you like to be
. This is a really healthy
e aware that there can
still hope for a perfect

You can be a bit of a **pessimist**. Don't just
assume that things aren't going to work out
the way you want them to. Instead, try to have
a brighter outlook. It might feel a little awkward at first, but it will start to become more
natural the more you do it. Plus, you might be
surprised. If you think things will end well, they
often do!

0–5

6–

Answers

You're a total **optimist**! You tend to look on the bright side of things and assume that, in the end, everything will work out. That's why you aren't surprised when it does! While it doesn't feel natural, sometimes you should think ahead about what could go wrong. That way you'll be prepared instead of being caught off-guard.

You tend to be **rea'**
you think a situatio
expect the best. O'
prepared for the w
outlook to have! Yc
be problems, but y
outcome.

Destiny Awaits

Ever wonder what you'd see if you looked into a crystal ball? To see what the future holds for you, choose a path through the magical maze. Where you come out at the end will provide a clue to what's going to happen down the road.

START

Answers

Did you come out of the ♣ **exit?** You're going to have a very bright future. Things will just work out for you—whether you're catching a fly ball in a championship softball game or nailing a part for the school play—but you'll need to work hard, too.

GIRL TIME
A PLAY BY
RUBY WRITE

MMXII

Did you come out of the ✹ **exit?** You're going to be famous! It may not be for acting or singing, but you're going to accomplish something amazing in your life that will have everyone knowing your name. Work on your paparazzi smile!

Did you come out of the ☺ **exit?** Your life is going to be full of happiness. You'll always be surrounded by lots of friends, and you'll feel upbeat and excited about all the possibilities that await you.

Answers

Do you have **more sets of eyes** than anything else? You're a visual person and enjoy gazing at art and examining the way things look. In one glance you can take in more information than most people. You might tend to sit back and watch other people make decisions rather than taking charge yourself. If so, try helping lead some of the time. It's only fair to share the responsibilities.

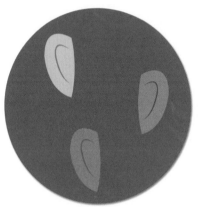

Do you have **more sets of ears** than anything else? You're a great listener! People like to ta you because they know you're really paying a tion. While this is a wonderful trait to have, r sure you speak up and say what's on your mi sometimes. You can't expect people to kno what you're thinking if you don't tell them.

Do you have **more lips** than anything else? You're great at speaking your mind. You know how to put words to your feelings and aren't afraid to say them out loud. Make sure you let others get in some talk time, too. You don't want to come across as someone who doesn't listen to other people's ideas.

Do you have an **even mix of eyes, ears, and lips?** You're great at expressing you in lots of different ways. Sometimes you need to talk, sometimes listen, and so times just observe. This works out in your favor since you can tailor your behav different situations.

Sense of You

Do you tend to use your eyes, ears, or lips more? For each of the questions below, draw the designated feature on the head if the answer is yes. In addition to drawing a funny face, you'll discover which sense is the strongest and learn if you're usually watching, listening, or talking.

Do you like taking pictures?
If yes, draw a set of **eyes** on the head.

Do you get a lot of phone calls?
If yes, draw a set of ears on the head.

Do you try out for parts in the school play?
If yes, draw a pair of **lips** on the head.

Are you good at putting outfits together?
If yes, draw a set of **eyes** on the head.

Do people call you quiet?
If yes, draw a set of ears on the head.

Do people say you talk a lot?
If yes, draw a pair of **lips** on the head.

Do you like going to museums?
If yes, draw a set of **eyes** on the head.

Do you love listening to music?
If yes, draw a set of ears on the head.

Do you raise your hand a lot in class?
If yes, draw a pair of **lips** on the head.

Do you watch a lot of movies?
If yes, draw a set of **eyes** on the head.

Do you try to listen in on other conversations?
If yes, draw a set of ears on the head.

Do you let secrets slip?
If yes, draw a pair of **lips** on the head.

Miss Independent

When it's safe to do so, it can be exciting to strike out on your own and express your individuality. Still, it can also be a little scary. The scariness is why a lot of girls go along with their friends on most decisions instead of making up their own minds. Follow the instructions to see which path you follow—your own or everyone else's.

Tomorrow is the first day of school and you haven't decided on an outfit yet. What do you do?

Color a square **purple** if you spend 30 minutes mixing and matching everything in your closet.

Color a square **green** if you do a fashion show in front of your parents to see what they like best.

Color a square **orange** if you call at least three friends to find out what they are wearing.

When filling out a class request form for the upcoming school year, which of the following do you do?

Color a square **purple** if you list the classes that sound most interesting to you.

Color a square **green** if you find out what classes your friends are signing up for, but ultimately choose ones that interest you most.

Color a square **orange** if you copy your best friend's class list exactly.

There's a dance coming up at school. What do you do?

Color a square **purple** if you love to dance and see no reason why you wouldn't go.

Color a square **green** if you make solemn vows with your friends not to leave each other's sides.

Color a square **orange** if you decide to skip it— you'd be so embarrassed if you were left all alone while your friends were off dancing.

If your parents moved and you had to start over at a new school, how would you feel?

Color a square **purple** if you'd feel a touch nervous but more energized—so many new people to meet!

Color a square **green** if you'd feel sad, but also excited for a fresh start.

Color a square **orange** if you'd be really upset that you had to leave all your friends and familiar places.

When given a choice, how do you pick which summer camp to attend?

Color a square **purple** if you think about a hobby that you want to get better at.

Color a square **green** if you sign up for the same one as last year.

Color a square **orange** if you choose whichever one your sister is attending.

Your favorite teacher is looking for one volunteer to stay after school and help with a project. How do you respond?

Color a square **purple** if you immediately raise your hand—it sounds fun!

Color a square **green** if you wait to see if anybody else volunteers. If not, raise your hand.

Color a square **orange** if you keep quiet—you don't like doing things by yourself.

While shopping with friends, you see a dress that you love, but your friends think it's ugly. What do you do?

Color a square **purple** if you buy it anyway because you know you can make it work.

Color a square **green** if you decide to think about it and come back later if you still want it.

Color a square **orange** if you say that you were kidding and that you think it's ugly, too.

Some of your friends start acting mean toward another girl. What do you do?

Color a square **purple** if you continue being nice to her—she didn't do anything to you.

Color a square **green** if you tend to avoid her so that you don't have to pick a side.

Color a square **orange** if you join in on the jokes—you don't want to be the next one to be singled out.

Answers

S.S. VERY INDEPENDENT

Miss Very Independent If you colored in more purple squares, you have a strong independent streak. You tend to not really care what others think about your actions, and you make decisions based on what you want to do. While this is good because you stay true to yourself, make sure you don't ignore other people's feelings. It's nice to compromise sometimes if it helps someone else out.

S.S. KIND OF INDEPENDENT

Miss Kind of Independent If you colored in more green squares, you can be independent at times, but it takes some extra effort. You usually know what you want to do in any given situation, but you like to check in with some of your friends before taking action. If you feel awkward going against what other people are doing, remember that being unique is better than disappearing into the crowd!

S.S. NOT SO INDEPENDENT

Miss Not So Independent If you colored in more orange squares, you are much more comfortable going along with the crowd than standing out in it. You tend to follow what your friends do, but this sometimes means you ignore your own interests or desires. Remind yourself that true friends won't stop liking you if you do something without them. If anything, they'll love that you're staying true to yourself and will find you even cooler.

Pressure Pro

Knowing how to act when the going gets rough will help you deal with anything life throws at you. Using only squares, triangles, and circles, draw any type of animal you'd like. Then turn to the answer key to find out what it means about how you react to tough times.

Answers

If you made an animal that can run fast, you like to get through things as quickly as possible. You decide on a solution and do it—you don't like to waste time. Keep in mind that if you think about it a little longer, there could be another solution that might work better!

If you made an animal that lives in the ocean, you are graceful under pressure and help people find a solution that works for them. You're the person people turn to because you keep your head about you and make sure everyone is happy with the outcome. It can be fun to help others, but don't forget about making sure you're happy, too!

If you made an animal that flies, you don't let pressure get to you at all. You soar over hard times and stay happy, no matter what. If you do find yourself feeling overwhelmed or sad, that's OK, too. Just remember that those times will pass.

If you made an animal that can be a pet you could sleep with, you like to let others handle the decision making. It's fine to sit back and let other people lead you to a solution, but don't be afraid to speak your mind either. Problems are fixed faster when everyone helps out.

What to Do

From a deck of cards, pull out a queen, a king, and a joker. Mix up these three cards and lay them facedown in a row. Then just flip the cards over one by one to come up with your perfect plan for a fun day.

Answers

The first card tells you what activity to do:

JOKER: Draw a picture. Pick a subject—a vase of flowers, your bedroom, or a pet—and sketch it. If you have a tough time making the drawing look realistic, remember that there's no wrong way to make art!

QUEEN: Write a story. Using a recent event or a figment of your imagination, create a detailed tale. Help your readers see the people and places as clearly as you do—so be specific! Don't forget to tie it up with a clever title.

KING: Read. Select a story—an old fave or a library discovery. Find a comfy chair and escape into a different world, learn about a famous person, or travel in time. When you're done, ask your parents about their recent reads.

The second card tells you what to quiz your family about:

JOKER: Ask a family member to tell you his or her most embarrassing stories.

QUEEN: Ask a family member about a person—famous or not—that he or she most admires.

KING: Ask a family member to describe a moment when he or she felt super proud of himself or herself. And don't forget to give your own answer!

The third card tells you what kind of yummy snack to make:

JOKER: Veggie time. Raid the crisper drawer or counter for baby carrots, cucumber slices, cherry tomatoes, pepper slices, etc. Try a favorite salad dressing as a dip.

QUEEN: Salty and sweet. Spread peanut or almond butter on apple slices for a simple, yet sticky, treat.

KING: Mix it up. Create a DIY yogurt parfait by layering yogurt, berries, and crunchy cereal or granola in a bowl.

Two of a Kind

This activity is fun to do with your best friend! In the diagram on the next page, write your name at the top and your friend's name at the bottom. Then go down the list of words and write the word in your section if it describes only you, in your BFF's section if it describes only her, and in the middle section if it describes both of you. If the word doesn't describe either of you, skip it and move on to the next word.

fearless

cautious

cheerful

excitable

energetic

sporty

funny

chatty

helpful

loud

quiet

playful

punctual

outgoing

responsible

shy

silly

serious

caring

stylish

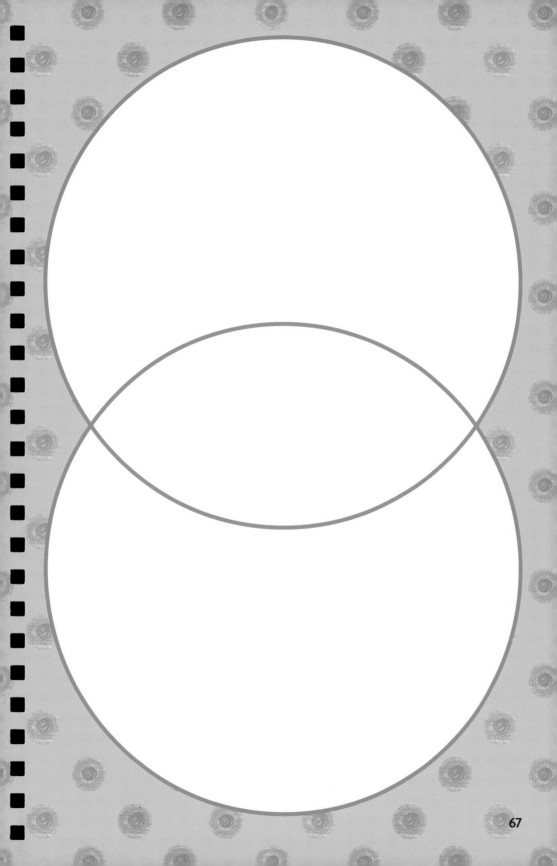

Answers

Having **three or fewer words listed in the middle** means you like hanging out with people completely different from you. This is good because you'll always be challenged and will constantly learn new things about yourself. It also shows that you don't mind getting to know people with whom you may not have much in common. You know that what's important is a person's character, not whether you both like the same hobbies.

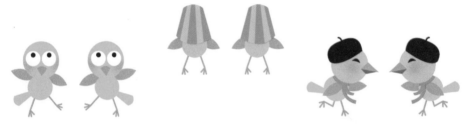

Having **four to six words listed in the middle** means you enjoy sharing some interests with your friends. You tend to like hanging out with people who are up for trying new things together. This means that whenever you want to try a new hobby, such as joining the swim team, starting a book club, or going camping, at least one of your friends is going to want to do it with you.

Having **more than six words listed in the middle** means you seek out people really similar to you. You like knowing that your friends are always going to be up for the same things you are—you think life is more fun that way! That's why you'll always have a big group with you when you go to the mall, try out for basketball, or try your hand at jewelry making. With so much in common, you and your pals will be friends for life!

Puppy Play

Discover the best breed for you.

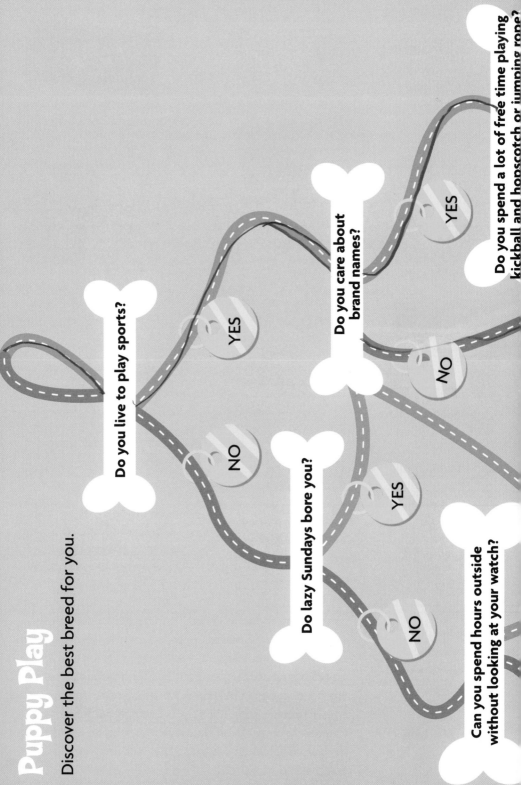

Do you live to play sports?

YES

NO

Do you care about brand names?

YES

NO

Do lazy Sundays bore you?

YES

NO

Can you spend hours outside without looking at your watch?

Do you spend a lot of free time playing kickball and hopscotch or jumping rope?

YES

ney Smarts

's your dollar sense?

all with $20 in your purse, you spend

→ some of it, no matter what.

of it, every single time.

The sale rack is the

only place you'd ever buy something.

last place you'd look—all the stuff there is old!

first place you check, before seeing what else is in the store.

r you lend your sister $10,

you remember she owes it to you but aren't too worried.

rget about it the next day.

It's almost the holiday season. For gifts, you

have enough money saved that you can get exactly what you want for everyone.

hadn't thought about them. Oops! You hope your dad will give you enough money to pay for what you want to get everyone.

erstar! You keep money treat yourself when tra. You know how don't think you need t something nice. cks are for!

You're a **big spender.** While it can be fun to buy things with your money, make sure to keep some in your piggy bank, too. Otherwise you won't have anything left when an emergency comes up (your headphones break) or it's a special occasion (a new dress for the dance). You don't have to save every penny, but start by putting 30 percent of whatever you get in an envelope out of sight. If it isn't in your wallet when you go to the mall, you won't be tempted to spend it!

If you go to the

a

none of it—you didn't see anything you loved.

When you think about how much money your parents spend, you

wish you had that much to spend.

get worried; it's too much.

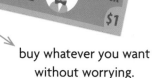

$20 TWENTY BUCKS $20

At

you write up an agreement and ask her daily where the money is.

If you started up a pet-sitting business, it would be so you can

$1 ONE BUCK $1

you

put more money in your savings toward college.

buy whatever you want without worrying.

You're **super frugal** and hate to spend money at all. While it's great to save for a rainy day, make sure you remember to treat yourself with your hard-earned money every now and then. The treat doesn't have to be anything huge, but a new tube of shimmery lip gloss or a book that will entertain you will help you feel good and won't use up all your savings.

You're a **saving s**
for savings but al
you have a little
to bargain shop a
to spend a lot to
That's what sales

NO   YES

sleepy

jackie

NO   YES

zippy

A **sleepy bulldog.** You like hanging out at home and relaxing, and this breed does, too. While all animals need some exercise, bulldogs can get by with shorter walks. Make sure to train him, though—he can have a lot of muscle, and you don't want him jumping up and scaring your friends.

An **energetic Jack Russell terrier.** This breed has a ton of energy, but so do you! Make sure to take her to the park and go on long walks with her as often as you can—she'll love you forever.

A **playful mutt.** You don't care that this pup isn't a purebred; you're just happy that he wants to run after a ball and play catch, and is up for any other kind of fun. See if your town has a park with a lake that dogs can swim in during certain hours—your mutt might just love the water!

Tell us which quiz was your favorite!

Write to
Personality Patterns Editor
American Girl
8400 Fairway Place
Middleton, WI 53562

(Sorry, but photos can't be returned. All comments
and suggestions received by American Girl may be
used without compensation or acknowledgment.)

Here are some other American Girl books you might like: